everything&

everything& ©2020 by **Ehlayna Napolitano**. Published in the United States by Vegetarian Alcoholic Press. Not one part of this work may be reproduced without expressed written consent from the author. For more information, please contact vegalpress@gmail.com

Cover art by Alicia Napolitano

Contents

everything&..3

if we can't even trust the babies,
who can we trust?
there is a line where preconception meets destiny,
i've seen it.

i have to remember to ask the clock
if she knows where we're going.
i wonder if everyone who's coming
is already here.

not sure yet if there's a way
to be honest and tender
together — facts are different than truth.

&&&

my bus to new york was very late and
a man next to me asked for a smoke
"you gotta smoke" he asked or said
and i said "what" like
i wasn't sure if it was a command or question

i didn't have any cigarette to give him
and he said it was ok,
he couldn't smoke on the bus anyway.

i was on my way to see c —
i like the way the air is so
much like clarity
outside their door.

&&&

oh, it's so gentle, so gentle,
this is going to help me

i think i'll have
        an answer for you, soon,

and for now
i understand that offering blankets to m
when she sleeps on my couch
is the same as building a house.

&&&

i cut my bangs
in my bathroom in denver
and when I get back she says i look like
some kind of mountain

by that i think she means
wild,
but probably more like
insurmountable

&&&

at my feet this morning were
two doves. one was dead
and the other plucked feathers from
its body.

that which homes you
you create. in a blinding fury
of tenderness, you force existence
out of the world.

&&&

certain things you can give to yourself.
very curious
how many spare changes accumulate
at the end of a long trip

i give them out like party favors for my friends,
the kind of things you want or need,
calmness as candied almonds, gentleness as a
disposable camera

and when i think about giving names to feelings,
i remember being small.

&&&

sleep tight, sleep tight,
one, every, all together
in the pinkish hue of the broken streetlight
on the block behind mine

&&&

is it there yet for you, j,
can you think of yourself as
satisfied,
now, now,

don't cry

&&&

should i remember every day that someone died

&&&

people let you forget little tragedies
   because certain things belong only to you

&&&

men have such loud eyes
they can scream me silent so easily

i feel my posture change under that echoing leer
and i'm never sure if i'm
shrinking or showing off

&&&

am i smiling or
baring my teeth when i
tell the man who groped me
that i am happy his new job is going
so well?

&&&

there is no way to write "i see your violence"
but i know you know it

&&&

performative smallness, like
i can use my hands to

reform the cracked places into smooth surfaces —

i want to ask him for permission
to eat my own hand, to take out my eyes and
save myself; deny what is before me and call it religion.

i keep acting like
i have something to say and then giving over
the unblemished version of my face
that bleeds so ugly, i
now spare him from it.

&&&

does w ever think about
that time

i stood yelling in the grass, looking
at the brick buildings and
lolling my tongue down to lick the dirt off my shoes

he told me it was beautiful,
and gave me water to soothe my
dry mouth.

&&&

it is at this point that r looks at me
and teaches me a lesson in how to be as tender as
freshly tilled soil —

it is night, and as we're sitting watching d climb a tree
he has climbed before,

the first act of kindness and the

ways events are tied to locations on the earth, how
we stand so often in the locations of
other people's monuments — i
wonder if she thinks of it the same way.

"we use to live here" she says
        and i think we still do —

&&&

what if i tell you all to do it
bend down to the river and
blow bubbles with your mouth until your
lips turn blue

sink your kiss into the claydirt, soft and red,
give back, give out, lay down in the moss
and sing love letters to the insects
as they claim your abandon for the earth

&&&

the man who drove me to the hotel told me that
i couldn't see the mountains because of the smoke
out west,

"the fires ate up the sky"
        he said,
"i love your violence"
        i said back.

&&&

she is saying something like
there is no way to peel yourself off the desk,

your open eyes burning from the
cleaning chemicals.

"is everything going to be all at once forever?" she says,
her eyes growing long and
papered over with times new roman type

and i am searing my mouth into the open position
to swallow it all down

&&&

venus flytraps are the easiest
of the carnivorous plants to grow
because they do not require much in the way of
particular planting conditions

however,
they are picky eaters and i read that if
you feed your venus flytrap a
dead bug, the soft jaws will not
close for the meal —
you must move the tiny body
around to simulate
life.

i think about the gruesomeness of
reanimating the dead beetle on my window,
which is frozen in the states before flying,
wings half out,
so
fragile;

what type of god steals a predator from its home
in the bog,

to smear dead bugs in its
fleshy maw?

&&&

at a certain point, it may feel
like there is nothing left to do but reach up between the branches
and yank free a peach and
eat it as you set fire to the tree it grew on

there is nothing more ungentle
than the moment of removal; however unsmooth the peach
in your hands,
the tree will grin queasily at you as it
burns.

&&&

my car crunched up and i am holding orange juice
i think i drank it,
i can't remember

m is sitting next to me, good in a crisis but
crying
my fault the tree is on fire,
my fault m lost her shoe,
my fault my elbow is bleeding,

and i think about how
tomorrow is w's birthday —

i think i am crying that the car kept us safe

but will now be crushed to small pieces of metal;
scrapped
for parts. funnel guilt into the broken window i
crawled out of
and reassure the woman bandaging my arm that i am
not normally like this.

&&&

how silly 14-year-old girls are.
when i was 14
my best friend took someone from her field hockey team
to buy a pregnancy test
and the boy i liked
was still playing basketball.

&&&

my closest encounter
to the ordinary ways the world mauls up its inhabitants
was my own fault —

don't cry

&&&

"how much sadder can it get"
i ask on the bathroom floor
and i'm holding my own tshirt in my hand,

the ghost that lives in my apartment
pats my sweaty head and says,
     "not much worse
       i promise"

&&&

"make it good, make it
        lovely" says d,
he is sitting cross-legged on my roof,

i can see the boys across the street sitting on
their roof   too,
        watching the night come at us and
seeing the explosions we call beautiful
because they come in primary colors.

connection is a funny thing; they
don't see me when i wave to them,

but i imagine that the silhouette of the one at the end is
thinking about
acceptable destruction
by the way he moves off the roof and back
inside.

&&&

muggy fog air always illustrates
a beer into my hand,
sweet weed smoke caught in my hair like
a syrup-swoon

i can feel the grass under me, aware
of the way the house before me is ill-formed, cheap
with plastic cups spilling out from every crevice,
and, at least once,
a door ripped totally in half —

where is s, i remember always

thinking — a certain point where there was
always gentleness, a fixed
constant as the room
swam.

&&&

there is a slight irregularity of unknown origin/if i am honest/

i'll be naming my heartbeats by the time i am old/if you know it you can make it known/irregularity as function/irregularity as cohesive/it all goes irregular/if you bellyflop too hard in a pool your skin will bruise and your body will rise from the water stranger, feeling changed/irregular/if you are taken in the airport and vanish without a trace/irregular/

is there a good time to tell your lover that you fear death/is it when you are smoking in bed/is it when they have just made you breakfast/is it after you have read their horoscope to them/

&&&

before it's too late, let's
call it two separate things — the
man and the
way we feel about the man.

is there a way to call it what it is that
does not grind against
Legacy? no —

a kitchen table,

burnt late-summer tomatoes on my plate;
an old woman telling me
family histories, or
the way
she remembered them, not the way
we tell them,

"let's not speak ill of the dead,"
        her daughter says to her, solemnly and
"i'm not"
she laughs, her age lines sinking into her skin as if
stalwart anchors against the glassiness of
purposeful smoothing,
        "this is how they were."

&&&

i do not mean to romanticize ophelia,
only to say that i understand
her —
standing with flowers, too many flowers in her hands, her
father
yelling "defilement!" like
a winning card in his,

of course it is a violent end she meets, her
corpse drenched in holy water, her
mouth open and blue
and maybe serene or maybe wailing —
her selfviolent finality,

is there any difference between a destroyed body
and a whole one if the decision of
completeness is not
borne of the body itself, but hurled ungracious

at it from some ungood father, railing
in anger?

&&&

there is no good place,
no good place to hold my hands so
softly, against the hard surfaces,

i want to teach them gentleness
smooth them to kind, bind them to the lesson
with my string and my teeth,
tying knots without help.

&&&

can i achieve the patience of a snail
moving as my child eyes watch its deliberate path
across the wooden barriers in the garden?

&&&

thinking about unsafety, like
the one time i had to run away from someone who
now knows where i live, because he
caught me, like an unsuspecting rabbit,
hopping out my front door one morning

i haven't seen him since but won't be
surprised to see him again, only feeling
familiar flashy fear
like i certainly can't fix it and how

embarrassed, how rattled i am by such a thing,
unaccustomed as i am to such

banal regularities

&&&

i am so obsessed with tenderness
because i am a cancer, and i like the way
your voice sounds when you say,
      "oh that makes sense"

&&&

if i can justify it, over and over, i'll
run my hands over it enough times;
      does this count as creation?

that sort of longing is
the place for me,
crisply aware but dimly
      lit.

&&&

the first cigarillo i ever had
was on what i remember to be the coldest night of january
in recent memory, which stretched back about
one week, for me.

i was standing up, my breath and smoke mixing visibly
in between me and c
and i remember thinking that i
had no idea if i was smoking right,
and c just laughed
and told me to hurry,
      it's so cold out here

&&&

(where / when / how)
       will i be warm
(can / should / will)
       i be warm

&&&

the last broadcast of a
self-help call-in show i used to listen to
ended rather unremarkably, with
the host counseling a woman
on the loss of her dog,

as it was ending, he told us that
he thanked us for listening and
as he always did, told us
"any chance to reach out is
       one less place you are alone."

&&&

yes, i think about you,
       is that what you need to hear?

&&&

b prefers things to be true,
to be teasable apart, to be grown as separate stalks
side by side.

he is trying to figure out how the vines of me
hang, when he is

telling me it will be okay,
when he is handing me my drink
and telling me it will be okay

&&&

she never hangs the art but wants to
pull it open and see its insides, its guts

she likes to yank the beating heart out and
take its pulse that way, still
vibrating with effort in her hand, the
blood in her fingers singing
to the blood spilling onto them

there it is, the moment of harmonious conception,
and she laughs and laughs and laughs

&&&

my sister is political.
radicalized in the expressive ether,
her hands are her pulpit as she pulls art from the nothingness,
it belongs to her.
how oppositional, to stand in the hypothetical
and become it real.

&&&

a wants to tell me about space
about how it unfolds on itself and how
funny it is to think about
the few things we know about it

"do you ever think about"
        she says to me as we're drinking tea
        on the porch one morning,
"how dark space is"
        and she bursts out laughing,
          unfurling in joyous unknowing

&&&

it's probably bullshit
that you can name a star after someone,
plus the star might already be dead,

a is right,
        i do think about space and its darkness and how
hilarious it all is

&&&

what a strange thing to think we can name anything at all

&&&

"how much worse can it get"
the ghost asks me as i'm chopping
onions in the kitchen

i wipe my hands on
my legs and turn on the tv,
        "not much worse,
          i promise"

&&&

the little placard on the wall

denoting a place where art used to hang
but doesn't any longer
is a love story

&&&

from here to there,
a teaching moment,

the birds know how to mourn,
i remind myself as i yank up the carpet,

not sure if that means they know
they're birds though,
i counter, tugging on the pieces that stay fastened,

the concept of mourning is a
conversation,
like when he asks, "how are you"
but doesn't mean he wants
to know about the hours

&&&

i'm going to ask r
if she knows how to clean a wound
and if she can teach me,

i think she might know because
it is an act of healing and every time i
have been sad, i have looked at her hands and known
they were good.

she knows how to make,
and what is a wound but something to make

new.

&&&

do not stitch my broken skin together/sear it up and burn me closed/rebirth me with absent sharpness/i want to be smooth/i want to be smooth/i want to close up/i want to not spill/i want to warm/i want to be warm/liquid me/smooth me/disremember me/i read that caterpillars retain their memories when they are disassembled and reassembled to a butterfly they can learn and their cells retain the memory/can i be like that/can i remember/can i remember/can i remember

&&&

where's a good place for the things i want to be?
can i call you by your first name?
is there wifi in here?
should i move at the end of the year?
can you hear me if i talk a little louder?
could i bring you down with me?
do i seem like the type of person to do that?
am i what he called me?
can you see me if i can see you?
should i bring a light jacket to this bar?
am i what she called me?
don't you have someplace to be?

&&&

much more than i encounter sweetness
i imagine it

head on my dash, you're screaming
that you want to be alive,

don't crash this car,
i want to be alive,

i can taste you in the shower after you go;
lap up the condensation and scream
that i want to hold you

i am so in love with you when you
jolt out of bed to see who is screaming on the street,
pulling on your shirt, yelling down,
who needs help

"why are you looking at me like that?"
        you ask,
and i tell you that you
        move so fast to be gentle.

&&&

i light
the tip of a tender cigarette and place it in
my mouth, this is an intimate act.

we are walking in the cold and
a flame on the lip is a measured expedience —

we must trust there is an extinguishing
 we will feel as
        an entryway,
        a place to be warm.

&&&

i am leveling my sword
at the men who
collar themselves in green.

immolation by the flints of their teeth
as silver and gold and copper
spark as they spill from their
mouths.

can stone match my steel?

&&&

i don't think i'm interested in
what they want me to do when they tell me to hold it in

the billboards keep saying that i should order in
the people at work think i'm going to get married

i keep laughing at the worst times
sliding my fingers over the lock and asking
"what time do you open?"

it's hard to think of someone as funny if you know them
i'm no longer interested in trading in pain

&&&

s and i are smoking in the rain,
giving names to the fog rising off the lake
and the birds darting back and forth —

> i've never felt as close to beauty
> as i am with tears in my eyes, s laughing and
> telling me how much he loves, how big it all is,

how everywhere the bird flies.

&&&

at the end of the world
i'm hoping to remember how
to get a butterfly to crawl onto my fingers

for no other reason
than to see its sunset wings before dark.

&&&

m and i are equally surprised
that the outlined carvings
of our adolescence
(are/are not) still crisp.

the steady erosion
of memory,
deliberate erasure more violent,
a place the memories go,

i still remember and
m and i are sitting above it, calling out
each of the ways we are
different than how we remember ourselves,

it exists as we piece it together,
a gentle hand guiding mine to the places
where things fit together, mine on hers too,
it is awfulsoft, grown together
gentle and forgotten and foundation.

&&&

when i am drinking my coffee
on the cement outside my office job
i am listening to the crickets discussing the weather
unbothered by the way my feet brush the tall grasses
they hum in.

i am lulled to sleep by the vibration of my phone
in the sheets beside me,
my friends cozily stroking my hand

"how about the way the cicadas are screaming"
        c asks me
"i know,
       i know,
              i hear them" i say

&&&

i'm finally starting to
refer to my body as an old apartment,
and not the wide-eyed painting that i see
above the sink at night,
so bleary and askew —

where the electrical sockets are and how to
push my belongings back into their neat places,
carved out and smooth with wear,

i know about the ways to live inside it,
the key under the mat

&&&

what about the complicated violence we do
to the home,
the way my hair is swirled in the drain and it
clogs up the water around my feet
or

the places where i have burned memory
straight onto the walls themselves,
like where we kissed on the floor on the first night here,

there are ways to turn something you want
into a way to get back at yourself.

&&&

maybe my childhood home will be subsumed by fire,
maybe it already has. i don't keep up
on news from my old address or
drive by very often.

press face to glass in a moving car,
take note of new flowers, an added porch, the kids toys
visible from the street —

an old woman who once lived in my house
dropped by a few years ago and asked to walk around.
her husband,
who had built the house up around them for years,
had died. and here she was,

she touched the places
we had torn down the wallpaper, looked
in on my CD collection
and my sister's stuffed animals, piled on her bed,

telling my mother how different it looked,
the gardens we'd grown.

&&&

where did i learn to hurt myself?
there is no animal compulsion
that calls for warped craving,
no wolf who calls to another to bite its ear,
for the pure joy of knowing death as an appetizer, so

what taught me to become a meal?
always wanting to be swallowed up, devoured, but
not savored,

i ask for the hit, i ask for the blows i have no name for
and when i get what i want,
the wolf howls hard and steady and i am
the bait, the trap, the hunter, the prey.

&&&

enough of metaphors, i want to talk,

talk about this, the way
  i sit with s in the park and
  drink a beer in the summer.

i think there is a place for this, the
gentle prodding of a coming thunderstorm
when a friend is sprawled in the grass —

the certain kind of destruction
that a placid day undone reflects; nothing
terrible, simply

   interrupted.

&&&

e has the best laughter,
  and she touches my face
  and tells me it will be okay,

reach for an indulgence
and call it by a new name.

&&&

i remember driving down the unlit road,
my headlights swinging around corners and
your voice coming through the engine;

i'd like to meet you where i think you are,
in your socks on the side of the road,
thinking about the places the sun melts my hands
into your face:

i know how to get there
  and always have.

&&&

the benign pull of
thinking i am the same —

i feel in love
at least three times a day
and sometimes i think of the mirror as the wand
to blow bubbles through,

like i'll get swallowed into containment
and push only gently on the outer limits.

&&&

maybe you will see me the way i do
        but i am not convinced of a hard line
between perception and projection —

i keep waking up with the phrase "there's not a place"
playing like a stuck cassette tape,
        skipping back to the beginning again and again,

there might be a place, or maybe not —
pushing on edges, and
        there i am.

&&&

i am still haunted by the woman who did not exist,
who d and j insisted was not there,
but the way her mouth lilted open and her
eyes as big as the windows i saw them through
        i think of her so often
        and have seen her every time
        i have not stopped to help.

&&&

it's probably a good time to mention
the ghost who lives in my apartment,
since as i write
        the ghost is
        sputtering about the audacity of fruit to wither,

    the way the mice nibble
    at the plants on my windowsill,
    how often they smell their mother in this
    old house,
        mint leaves and roll-on perfume and
        ash,

at the end of summer, i open the windows
and let the cool air rush in
to breathe the city back into the place i live,
and i bake things i don't want to eat,
    for the smallest mercy of triggering a memory —

and the ghost returns all my socks
that i didn't need during their missing period, anyway.

&&&

i am nearly done with my time
with this apartment but
    i feel confident
    that i will always be offering kindnesses
    to ghosts.

&&&

the existing time
is like the crack under my door that i dare
to see feet through every night — still
fearing to be alone, i see —

if i die bloody, no less unexpected than a demise
of softening visibility, of malleable timelines —
perhaps a more human death,
with someone acknowledging that i am alive

and then am not.

&&&

s is asking me if i will move
impulsively, love as a lover spills,
write about peaches —
        yes, i think i will.

&&&

and a note to self for when we die/i certainly am a flower/and make it a morning glory/my grandmother's bare feet in the grass alongside mine and there was still dew on the grass because the sun was barely up so the blades were sticking to my legs/her hands/my hands/she was holding the flower in her hand on the vine and showing me how it opens and closes/my mother always says i have her hands/very small/enough to hold a flower/enough to hold myself/i am certainly the flower i am holding/opening and closing/do i not grow/do i not vine/do i not offer beauty/flowers are hardcoded to unfurl/is a flower not certain/is a flower not sure/if so then make me a flower/forget a burial and point me toward the sun

Ehlayna Napolitano is a writer and editor living in Providence, Rhode Island. She is the author of *Penelope in the Morning* (tenderness lit, 2018). When she's not writing, she's most likely making a playlist dedicated to a niche feeling. Song recommendations can be sent to @ehlaynanaps on Twitter.

Lightning Source UK Ltd.
Milton Keynes UK
UKHW011836200520
363522UK00001B/113